For Susan, Carolyn, and Melia, who took this walk with me

For information about permission to reproduce selections from this book,
please contact permissions@astrapublishinghouse.com.

Calkins Creek
An imprint of Astra Books for Young Readers,
a division of Astra Publishing House
astrapublishinghouse.com
Printed in Canada

ISBN: 978-1-6626-8155-4 (hc)
ISBN: 978-1-6626-8154-7 (eBook)
Library of Congress Control Number: 2025943332

First edition

10 9 8 7 6 5 4 3 2 1

Design by Melia Parsloe
The text is set in Minnie Hand and Arquiteca.
The titles are hand lettered by Millie von Platen.
The illustrations are done digitally.

ZOHRAN

WALKS NEW YORK

MILLIE VON PLATEN

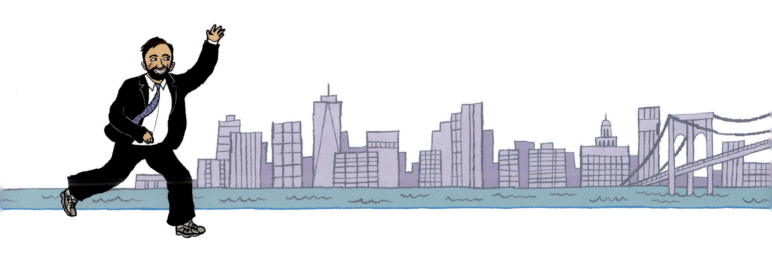

CALKINS CREEK
AN IMPRINT OF ASTRA BOOKS FOR YOUNG READERS
New York

Zohran has walked the streets of New York
ever since he was a child.

In Zohran's city, there are new things to do at every crosswalk.

And at every corner, new adventures waiting to be had—like a ferry ride.

This is where you come to cheer on the home team—

a ball game at Citi Field.

This is where you come to do hard things—

the icy waters of Coney Island.

And this is where you come to share joy—

on the subway to somewhere special.

In Zohran's city, everyone is always on the move!

But with *so* much to see and do . . .

. . . it can be hard to keep up.

Zohran knows when to slow down and listen.

Do you hear that?

It's neighbors welcoming you home
after a long walk.

This is Zohran's home, and it's yours, too.

ZOHRAN'S NEW YORK

Zohran Walks New York was inspired by Zohran Mamdani's thirteen-mile mayoral campaign walk from the end to end of Manhattan, Inwood Hill Park to Battery Park. In this book, Mamdani walks through all five boroughs, visiting real places that are special to him.

Mamdani was born in 1991 in Uganda. At age five his family moved to South Africa; two years later, when he was seven, they came to the UPPER WEST SIDE in MANHATTAN.

Mamdani is noted for eating his way through the city. At a halal food truck in ZUCCOTTI PARK, MANHATTAN, he not only grabbed some biryani, but he also advocated for fair food prices.

Mamdani advocates for accessible public transportation and especially enjoys the STATEN ISLAND FERRY, which is free for all to ride.

Mamdani is a fan of the Mets, who play at CITI FIELD in FLUSHING, QUEENS.

On New Year's Day in 2025, Mamdani took the Polar Bear Plunge at CONEY ISLAND in BROOKLYN. He called for freezing rents while wading in the icy water.

When Mamdani married Rama Duwaji, an artist, they rode the N and 4 trains from ASTORIA, QUEENS, to CITY HALL in MANHATTAN.

Mamdani has roots in the BRONX, where he attended THE BRONX HIGH SCHOOL OF SCIENCE.

Mamdani is a champion of the environment and green spaces, like ASTORIA PARK in QUEENS.

Mamdani is a New Yorker who embraces all the different people who call the city home. ASTORIA, QUEENS, where he lives, is one of the city's most diverse neighborhoods.

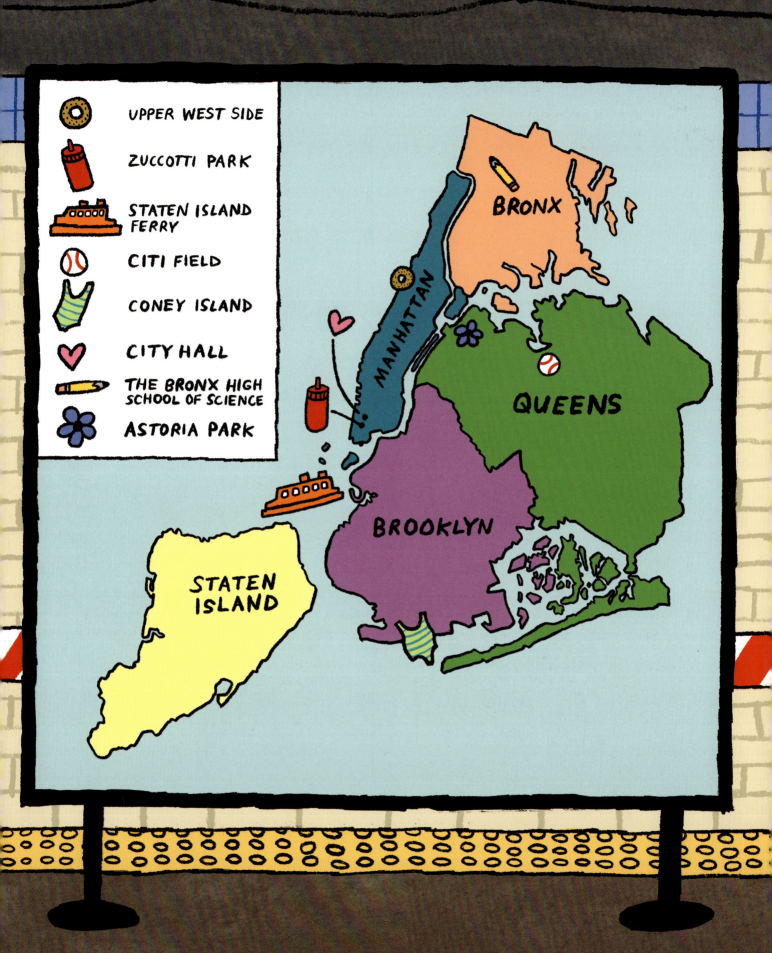